Absolute Relativism

The New Dictatorship and What to Do about It

Chris Stefanick

Catholic Answers Press
San Diego
2011

Absolute Relativism
Chris Stefanick
© 2011 by Catholic Answers, Inc.
15 14 13   4 5 6 7

Published by Catholic Answers, Inc.
2020 Gillespie Way
El Cajon, California 92020
1-888-291-8000 orders
619-387-0042 fax
catholic.com

Cover by Devin Schadt
Interior design by Russell Design
ISBN 978-1-933919-46-1

For my wife, Natalie, whose life is a pursuit
of Beauty and Truth. Without you I could do none
of what I do and I'd be half the man I am.

FOREWORD

In his 2010 Christmas address to the College of Cardinals, the Roman Curia, and the Governorate of Vatican City State, Pope Benedict XVI spoke clearly and strongly about the profoundly disordered moral state in which our world finds itself. Speaking about the grave evils of our time—for example, the sexual abuse of minors by the clergy, the marketing of child pornography, sexual tourism, and the deadly abuse of drugs—he observed that they are all signs of "the tyranny of mammon which perverts mankind" and that they result from "a fatal misunderstanding of freedom which actually undermines man's freedom and ultimately destroys it."[1]

His words are redolent of the powerful pastoral concern that he expressed in his homily during the Mass for the Election of the Roman Pontiff, celebrated before the conclave during which he was elected to the See of Peter. He spoke of how the "the thought of many Christians" has been tossed about, in our time, by various "ideological currents," observing that we are witnesses to the "human deception and the trickery that strives to entice people into error," about which St. Paul wrote in his Letter to the Ephesians.[2] He noted that, in our time, those who live according to "a clear faith based on the Creed of the Church" are viewed as extremists, while relativism—that is, "letting oneself be 'tossed here and there, carried about by every wind of doctrine'"—is extolled.[3] Regarding the source of the grave moral evils of our time, he concluded: "We are building a dictatorship of relativism that does not recognize anything as definitive and whose ultimate goal consists solely of one's own ego and desires."[4]

Reflecting once again, in his 2010 Christmas address, on the grave evils that are destroying us as individuals and as a society and have left us with a culture marked by violence and death, the Holy Father reminded us that, if we, with the help of God's grace, are to overcome these grave evils, "we must turn our attention to their ideological foundations."[5] He then identified directly and unequivocally the ideology that fosters these evils: a perversion of *ethos*, the norm of life or moral norm, which has even entered into the thinking of some theologians in the Church.

Referring to one of the more shocking manifestations of the ideology—namely, the so-called moral position that the sexual abuse of children by adults is actually good for the children and for the adults—he declared:

> It was maintained—even within the realm of Catholic theology—that there is no such thing as evil in itself or good in itself. There is only a "better than" and a "worse than." Nothing is good or bad in itself. Everything depends on the circumstances and on the end in view. Anything can be good or also bad, depending upon purposes and circum-

stances. Morality is replaced by a calculus of consequences, and in the process it ceases to exist.[6]

Pope Benedict XVI describes a moral relativism—called proportionalism or consequentialism in contemporary moral theology—that has generated profound confusion and outright error regarding the most fundamental truths of the moral law. [7] It has led to a situation in which morality itself "ceases to exist."

One thinks, for instance, of the plague of procured abortion in our society, which justifies the wholesale murder of the unborn in the womb as the exercise of the so-called right of the mother to choose whether to bring to term the baby she has conceived; of the artificial generation of human life and its destruction at the embryonic stage of development, which are justified as the means to find cures for crippling or deadly diseases; and of the so-called "mercy killing" of those who have the first title to our care—our brothers and sisters who have grown weak through advanced years, grave illness, or special needs—which is justified as care for the quality of their lives. One also thinks of the ever-advancing agenda of those who want to redefine marriage to include the unnatural sexual union of two persons of the same sex, which is justified as tolerance of so-called alternative forms of human sexuality, as if there were a true form of human sexuality other than that intended by God, our Creator and Redeemer.

To confront the ideology, Pope Benedict XVI has urged us to study anew the teaching of his predecessor, the Venerable (soon to be Blessed) Pope John Paul II, in his encyclical letter *Veritatis Splendor*, "On the Fundamentals of the Church's Moral Teaching," in which he, in the words of Pope Benedict XVI, "indicated with prophetic force, in the great rational tradition of Christian ethos, the essential and permanent foundations of moral action."[8] Reminding us of the need to form our consciences in accord with the moral teaching of the Church, our Holy Father also reminds us of "our responsibility to make these criteria audible and intelligible once more for people today as paths of true humanity, in the context of our paramount concern for mankind."[9] In the exhortation of Pope Benedict XVI, we see the expression of the deepest pastoral charity of the Vicar of Christ on earth: charity, which like that of the Christ the Good Shepherd, knows no boundary and is unceasing.

The book that you now hold in your hands is precisely a tool by which to respond to Pope Benedict XVI's exhortation that we must address the ideology that underlies so many and grave evils in our time. Through his writing, Christopher Stefanick—drawing upon his studies of the Church's moral teaching and his many years of working with the pastors of the Church, especially in their care of youth—helps us to reflect more deeply on "the concept of *ethos*," the moral norm, and its relationship to the unchanging truth about God, ourselves, and our world. Our author leads us to an ever deeper reflection upon our own moral thinking and its coherence with the moral truth that our Lord Jesus Christ teaches us in the Church. In a particular and most important way, he helps us to address a false notion of tolerance, which is nothing less than an expression of the "dictatorship of relativism," which threatens to destroy us and our society and through which morality "ceases to exist."

In the end, as our author reminds us, we discover the truth, the true concept of *ethos*, in Jesus Christ in a personal relationship with him as he comes to meet us and to make us ever more one with him in his Mystical Body, the Church. In Jesus Christ, God the Son made man, heaven has come to earth to dispel the darkness of error and sin and to fill our souls with the light of truth and goodness. If we live in Christ, in the union of our hearts with his Sacred Heart, to use the words of our author, "when people who are choking on the fumes of relativism come near [us], they should get a whiff of the rarified air of heaven and a glimpse into a world that makes sense." Living in Jesus Christ, living in accord with the truth that he alone teaches us in his Church, we become light to dispel the confusion and error that lead to so many and grave moral evils of our time and to inspire a life lived in accord with the truth and, therefore, marked by freedom and joy.

Christopher Stefanick expresses his own confrontation of the ideology underlying the profoundly disordered moral state in which our world finds itself today by patiently and carefully leading us in carrying out the same necessary confrontation. Using an approachable question-and-answer method, he shows a sensitivity and an understanding of the struggle that we face in our culture to think clearly with Christ about moral truth. Having enjoyed the collaboration of Christopher Stefanick during a number of my years as Bishop of La Crosse, Wisconsin, I can assure you that his responses to the questions he raises in order to know and teach the truth about the moral law are heartfelt—that is, they are the fruit of his union of heart with the Sacred Heart of Jesus, especially in Christ's care for youth. In the name of all who will read and study our author's important writing on relativism, I express the deepest esteem and gratitude to him. In our gratitude, let us pray for God's continued blessing upon the important work of Christopher Stefanick in helping us all to fulfill "our responsibility to make [the essential and permanent foundations of moral action] audible and intelligible once more for people today as paths of true humanity, in the context of our paramount concern for mankind."[10]

It is my hope, as a shepherd of the flock, that Christopher Stefanick's work on moral relativism will inspire us all to undertake that new study of the encyclical letter *Veritatis Splendor* of the Venerable Pope John Paul II, which Pope Benedict XVI urges. Thus may we all, with the help of God's grace, overcome the grave moral evils of our time and transform our culture marked by violence and death into a culture of love and life. May Our Lady of Guadalupe, Mother of God and Mother of America, be the Star who leads us with deepest maternal love to her divine Son who alone is, for us, "the way, and the truth, and the life" (Jn 14:6).

Raymond Leo Cardinal Burke
Archbishop Emeritus of Saint Louis
Prefect of the Supreme Tribunal of the Apostolic Signatura
February 22, 2011: Feast of the Chair of St. Peter

1   Pope Benedict XVI, "Benedict XVI's Christmas Greeting to the College of Cardinals, the Roman Curia and the Governorate: Resolved in Faith and in Doing Good," *L'Osservatore Romano Weekly Edition in English*, December 22–29, 2010.

2   Cardinal Joseph Ratzinger, "Mass for the Election of the Roman Pontiff: Monday, 18 April: Homily by the Cardinal Who Became Pope," *L'Osservatore Romano Weekly Edition in English*, April 20, 2005. Cf. Eph. 4:14.

3   Ibid.

4   Ibid.

5   Pope Benedict XVI, "Benedict XVI's Christmas Greeting."

6   Ibid.

7   Cf. Pope John Paul II, encyclical letter *Veritatis Splendor* (On the Fundamentals of the Church's Moral Teaching), August 6, 1993, no. 75.

8   Pope Benedict XVI, "Benedict XVI's Christmas Greeting."

9   Ibid.

10 Ibid.

Got Truth?

Two thousand years ago, one man's question echoed in a hall in Jerusalem. "What is truth?" Pontius Pilate asked Jesus (Jn 18:38). That same question echoes in our hearts today. Is there really truth to be found when it comes to the most important things in life, or are we each just left with our own opinions? Can we know—for certain—why we exist, if life has any purpose, and what happens after we die? Can we know how we're supposed to live and if there is a God? And does claiming to know the truth about these things make someone intolerant?

So what is truth, anyway?

According to my friend Webster, truth is simply "the property of being in accord with fact or reality." The biggest obstacle to finding truth today—when it comes to those most important questions of faith, morals, and life's meaning—is relativism.

I've never even heard of relativism. What is it?

Cardinal Joseph Ratzinger (now Pope Benedict XVI) identified relativism as "the greatest problem of our time."[1] Considering the times in which we live, that's a big claim, and it's one we can't afford to ignore.

Relativism is the idea that there is no universal, absolute truth but that truth differs from person to person and culture to culture. In other words, truth is *relative* to what each person or culture thinks.

It seems that most people today are moral and religious relativists.[2] They think that only what can be scientifically verified should be regarded as objective fact but that everything else is subjective opinion. For instance, no one would say, "Two plus two equals four *for me* but it might equal five *for someone else*, and we're both correct." But people often say things like, "Christianity is true *for me*, while Islam is true *for someone else*," "You have your truth, and I have mine!" or "You can't impose *your* morality on someone else!"

We've all encountered relativism in statements like the ones above, but more importantly we've encountered relativism in the spiritual emptiness and moral free-for-all that occurs when people think there is no truth about who God is and how we are supposed to live—only a multitude of opinions. Many hold this "philosophy" without ever putting a name to it, and they end up separated from life's most important realities.

Relativism is so widespread that Ratzinger describes its predominance in our day as the "dictatorship of relativism."[3] And even though many never seem to have heard of it, relativism is considered necessary to preserve peace and equality in our diverse world. For instance, if someone claims that he can know the truth with certainty about a religious or ethical issue (that is, he is a "realist" as opposed to being a "relativist") and that those who disagree with him are "wrong," he is usually labeled "intolerant," "rigid," or "closed-minded."

Now that we've spelled out what relativism is, we're going to look at what makes it one of history's worst popular philosophies and why it is "the greatest problem of our time." We'll also see how belief in moral and religious truth leads to *real* tolerance, while relativism—contrary to popular belief—leaves us with a false tolerance at best and intolerance at worst. Most importantly, we're going to dig into how you can know *the* answers to life's most important questions: questions about faith, morals, and meaning.

What's the problem with relativism?

It's not difficult to show what's wrong with relativism. It's widely accepted only because it's rarely scrutinized. Since it has worked its way into the fabric of our society, it is simply assumed to be true. But one hard look at relativism reveals that it doesn't work as a philosophy or in real life.

How is relativism flawed as a philosophy?

The one "dogma" of relativism is that it is absolutely true for everyone that nothing is absolutely true for everyone. This claim can't be true because it contradicts itself—it's what we call a self-contradicting proposition. If it's true for everyone that nothing is true for everyone, then the statement "Nothing is true for everyone" also isn't true for everyone! (If you didn't get that last sentence, say it out loud a few times. It'll sink in!)[4]

Okay, but what if I'm just a relativist when it comes to faith and morals and not with things that can be proven by science?

Even with this clarification, relativism still contradicts itself. It says, "*Only* scientifically verifiable statements are absolutely true." But this claim is not scientifically verifiable.

Isn't this just philosophical semantics? What does it have to do with real life?

It has everything to do with how you approach life, how society forms itself, and whether or not we discover the most profound realities in life. Stay with me; you'll see how.

You said relativism doesn't work in real life. Why?

Relativists hold that there are no right and wrong moral choices; rather, right and wrong are *relative* to one's feelings, sentiments, or cultural milieu. But one look at moral atrocity shows us that this cannot be true. After the events of 9/11, New York City Mayor Rudolph Giuliani stood before world delegates at the United Nations and said, "We're right and they're wrong [to have attacked innocent people]. It's as simple as that. . . . The era of moral relativism . . . must come to an end. . . . There's no moral way to sympathize with grossly immoral actions."[5]

It would be impossible to watch burning bodies jumping from the Twin Towers and say, "Flying planes into those buildings was right *for the terrorists*, so who are we to judge their actions?" Some choices are clearly right and others clearly wrong. It's safe to say there were very few moral relativists in America on 9/11—at least for that one day.

Because it is impossible for relativism to be consistent, many people end up being "selective relativists," objective about things they feel strongly about (terrorism? gun control? global warming?) but nothing else (sexual ethics? religion?).

Can't we just agree that everyone can make up their own truth as long as they don't hurt anyone else?

Most relativists would tell you that each person can create his own right and wrong with the one rule that we shouldn't hurt or restrain anyone else. But as soon as someone admits a single *should* into his vocabulary, such as "We should not hurt anyone else" or "We *should* not impose our views on others," he has undermined moral relativism, where there are no objective moral standards. Furthermore, this one rule can't be guaranteed by relativists because it's not resting on anything but the popular opinion of the day.

I can see how it might be bad philosophy, but is relativism really hurting anyone?

I understand that at first glance relativism seems harmless or even helpful in a multicultural world, but Pope Benedict XVI is right: Relativism *is* the greatest problem of our time. The list of its bad effects is potentially endless. Forgive me for getting on my soapbox while I run through a few of them for you. (I promise I'll only be on there for a few pages.)

1. Relativism robs us of a sense of meaning.

In the words of Pope Benedict XVI to teens and young adults at World Youth Day 2008, "A spiritual desert is spreading: an interior emptiness, an unnamed fear, a quiet sense of despair."[6] This emptiness is the inevitable result of relativism, which separates us from life's most profound realities. This is, perhaps, its most tragic effect.

Science can answer questions about the matter of the universe but not questions about its meaning. Fundamental questions such as "Why do I exist?" "How am I supposed to live?" and "What happens when I die?" can be answered only by philosophy and theology. Because of this, the relativist would say that the answers to these questions aren't truths to be discovered but ideas that each person should make up for himself. In the end, this is an admission that life either has no inherent meaning or, if it does, we can't know it for sure.

Many relativists—driven by an inescapable need to live for *something*—come up with shallow conclusions about life's meaning. This gives rise to bumper-sticker "philosophies": "Volleyball is life!" "Skate or die!" or, in Wisconsin, "I bleed gold and green!" While it's good to discover one's gifts, passions, or favorite football team, such things do not ultimately answer the questions of life's meaning—but for many people, these are all they have. Others invent more profound purposes for themselves than mere hobbies or allegiances, but regardless of whether these purposes are deep or shallow, the relativist has to admit that he has not discovered the meaning of life but rather has created his own. However, we need more than make-believe about life's most important questions to have a real sense of meaning, hope, and security. We need solid answers.

Lack of a firm sense of purpose leads to either despair or the desperate attempt to avoid life's most important questions through endless distractions. Perhaps this is one of the causes of our rampant consumerism and incessant text messaging. Take, for example, record-setting Florida teen Emilee: She sent and received 35,463 text messages in a single month.[7] It's difficult to be silent and reflective if it means facing the reality that underneath it all is nothing at all.

Reflecting on the damaging effects of a relativist culture on the young, Pope John Paul II lamented:

False teachers, many belonging to an intellectual elite in the worlds of science, culture, and the media, present an *anti-gospel*. . . . When you ask them: What must I do?, their only certainty is that there is no definite truth, no sure path. . . . Consciously or not, they advocate an approach to life that has led millions of young people into a sad loneliness in which they are deprived of reasons for hope and are incapable of real love.[8]

Young people ask what the meaning of life is, who God is, and how they are to live and are left to make up their own answers. This leaves them with little more than volleyball or boyfriends who might break their hearts tomorrow. It is no wonder that, according to a recent Centers for Disease Control and Prevention survey, almost 15 percent of teens had seriously considered suicide, and almost 7 percent had actually tried it.[9] No doubt some of that is the sad result of mental illness, but a percentage that high represents a more far-reaching societal problem—a *crisis in meaning* and a *poverty of purpose*.

2. Relativism leaves us with no criterion for moral decision-making but personal taste.

Pope Benedict XVI said that "relativism, which recognize[s] nothing as definitive, leaves as the ultimate criterion only the self with its desires."[10] That is because relativism leaves us with no objective truths to govern our behavior. The moral compass of a relativist has nowhere to point but to himself.

When asked what sin is, then-President-elect Barack Obama summed up moral relativism beautifully by saying, "Being out of alignment with my values."[11] Note that he did not say, "Knowingly doing something *wrong*," because relativists don't believe in universal moral laws but only legitimately varying "values." (My intent isn't to pick on the 44th president of the U.S. He was merely able to articulate what many seem to think.)

A person who believes in objective moral truth approaches a moral dilemma and asks, "Is this action right or wrong?" A relativist, taught only to clarify his values, asks, "Do I *really* want to do this?" or "Will this action make me *feel* good or bad?" The golden rule of relativist ethics is not *do the right thing* but *do as you will*.[12]

Of course, the fact that relativism excuses us from living according to certain moral guidelines is one reason this philosophy has become so popular. It's also why it's so hard for many to part with.

It isn't difficult to see how making moral decisions based on our feelings and personal preferences can lead to disaster. Many people in jail did things that felt very good to them at the moment they committed their crimes, or they can tell you that they were acting in alignment with the values they had at the time. Likewise, countless young people suffer from the consequences of promiscuity and drug abuse, which felt good to them at the moment but left them in ruin.

3. Relativism deprives children of formation.

We no longer encourage young people to find and conform to the truth. Many are under the impression that a young person can discover who he really is only if he is "free" from the molds of his parents, society, religion, or even his own body.

In a recent example of relativism run amok, the parents of a seven-year-old "transgendered" boy "discovered" that he had a boy's body but apparently "a girl's brain." They sent him to school dressed as a girl, thinking that he'd find his true self by conforming to his confusion rather than what was dictated by his body.[13] The outcome of this situation is that a child in desperate need of counseling for gender-identity disorder is getting none. Here we see an extreme illustration of how we are raising a relativist generation.

When we offer our children acceptance without guidance or teach them ethics without reference to truth, far from setting them free, we are morally abandoning them. The sad irony is that this abandonment usually happens in the name of love. But love without truth—much like truth without love—is a unique form of cruelty.

Apply the principles of relativism to drivers education classes and see how misguided our relativist child-rearing is. Would we consider it loving acceptance to tell teens learning how to drive that they no longer had to pay attention to those silly yellow lines that repressed their forefathers and kept them in their lanes? Yet this is how we train young people in ethics, which deals with how they "drive" their lives. Left with moral compasses that are directed only by self-reflection and desire, countless young people drift into ruin. What many call loving acceptance is in fact moral abandonment, and there is nothing loving about it.

In the words of Pope Benedict XVI, "Only in truth does charity shine forth, only in truth can charity be authentically lived. . . . Without truth, charity degenerates into sentimentality. Love becomes an empty shell, to be filled in an arbitrary way. In a culture without truth, this is the fatal risk facing love."[14]

4. Relativism separates us from one another.

It isn't just blood relationships but rather ideals, principles, and traditions that unite a people and create a nation. When people rally around something bigger than themselves, they experience unity. Relativism removes the notion that we need to conform to a reality that is bigger than our own opinions, values, and preferences. It erodes the mortar that builds a society. Pope Benedict XVI has said that "under the semblance of freedom [relativism] becomes a prison for each one, for it separates people from one another, locking each person into his or her own ego."[15]

Relativism replaces *E pluribus unum* ("out of many, one") with *E pluribus pluribus* ("out of many, many").[16] Nothing has the power to dissolve a nation like relativism. Perhaps this will be proven in Western civilization over the next few hundred years, though I hope it isn't.

5. Relativism undermines the right to life.

Some will claim that there is nothing wrong with abortion. Our point isn't to debate that issue at length but simply to show how abortion could be legal only in a relativist society.

First, abortion is legal because of how a relativist society comes to see human rights. When a society acknowledges that human rights are based on objective principles—like the dignity of the person and natural law—those rights are secure. But a society that does not recognize moral assertions as objective facts puts those rights on shaky ground. Rights come to be regarded as favors granted by the state or by a majority vote. This is even the case with what was once seen as the inalienable right to life. "No rights are safe when the right to life is not."[17]

John Paul II saw the causal relationship of relativism to abortion very clearly. In *Evangelium Vitae* (The Gospel of Life), he wrote, "The original and inalienable right to life is questioned or denied on the basis of a parliamentary vote. . . . This is the sinister result of a relativism which reigns unopposed: the 'right' ceases to be such, because it is no longer firmly founded on the inviolable dignity of the person."[18]

Second, abortion is legal because of how a relativist society views "human wrongs." In the words attributed to Mother Teresa, "If abortion isn't wrong, what is?" For the relativist who carries his philosophy to its logical conclusion, the answer would be "Nothing is 'wrong.'"

One of the central arguments of pro-abortion groups is implied by the popular name of their movement: "pro-choice."[19] They claim that abortion should be legal in the name of "freedom of choice," not necessarily because it's a moral decision. Such an argument could win only in a society where no act is seen as inherently wrong and "freedom alone, uprooted from any objectivity, is left to decide by itself what is good and what is evil."[20]

Abortion was made legal by relativism and probably remains legal because of it.

Though polls show a majority of Americans are opposed to abortion, they do nothing about it—most likely because a majority of Americans are relativists, not wanting to "impose *their* morality" on someone else.[21] And so it seems that a multitude of Americans think an act is murder but won't do anything about it. This fact proves that we are able to turn a blind eye to any action if we think it falls under the protective umbrella of relativism. It isn't hard to see how this trend could be extremely dangerous.

Thanks to relativism, our societal trend regarding human life won't end with legalized abortion. We are doing things today that humanity would have found almost universally repulsive until just a generation ago. In the 1970s, *in vitro* fertilization was hotly debated, and Britain's Medical Research Council refused to fund research out of ethical and safety concerns. In 2010 one of the founders of IVF won a Nobel Prize.[22] Today human embryos are used to advance medicine, and British scientists are legally creating human-animal hybrid clones for experimentation. This too is debated, but it's legal nonetheless.

It is assumed that we *can* progress scientifically; however, there seems to be less and less regard for whether or not we *should*.

Science like this can no longer claim to be at the service of humanity. Rather, it puts human life at the service of science—or the helpless at the service of the wealthy and strong. Such "progress" is actually regress, a return to survival of the fittest. Life at its weakest is no longer safe when relativism reigns. Human rights are no longer treated as absolutes but rather are made subject to the "values" of those in positions of authority.

6. Relativism makes it easy for those in authority to manipulate others.

As we said above, when people don't think their rights are based on objective principles, they come to see them as favors granted by those in power. Such favors can just as easily be taken away by government authorities or a majority vote. In the words of Pope John Paul II, "To educate without a value system based on truth is to abandon young people to moral confusion, personal insecurity, and easy manipulation."[23]

The Founding Fathers of the United States weren't easily manipulated by those in power because they weren't relativists. They saw their rights as "inalienable"—moral facts firmly founded in man's very nature. They saw that a person's inherent dignity demanded self-governance. They were certain enough about their rights to be willing to die for them. If they had been relativists, America probably wouldn't exist today.

In words often attributed to Edmund Burke, "All that is necessary for evil to prevail is for good men to do nothing." Relativism produces a society of "do-nothings" in the face of moral evils. Why put your life on the line for your "personal values system"? Why resist unjust laws and authorities if there are no *real* rights but just varying preferences?

7. Relativism puts the freedom of speech under attack.

We can easily debate objective principles in math or science without worrying about hurting people's feelings or having our words labeled "hate speech," because these topics are recognized as belonging to the realm of fact. The subject matter is a step removed from us. But a relativist world equates moral decisions and religious creeds with personal sentiments that lack any objectivity. As a result, debating the validity of someone else's claims is often perceived as a nasty, personal attack. Perhaps this is why debates of a religious or ethical nature tend to quickly escalate to emotional battles devoid of logic. It seems we're losing our ability to intelligently debate the most important things! And worse, it's becoming ever more dangerous to do so.

In recent years it has become ever more precarious for institutions like the Catholic Church to teach some of the traditional ethics that it has taught and to which most of Western civilization has adhered for thousands of years. For instance, discussing the moral character of a sexual act is often labeled "bigotry" and "hate speech"—even if it is done charitably and respectfully (which it always should be).

We see real-life examples of this trend in Canada, where you can be sued for saying or writing anything that can "expose a person or persons to hatred or contempt" or, in other words, for strongly criticizing another's ideas or lifestyle.[24] The person doing the suing may have all legal fees covered by the state. The person being sued has to cover his own fees and has no right to face his accuser. Under this law (which can be used to beat those who subscribe to objective truth into submission), clergymen have been put through grueling and costly trials for defending traditional marriage or for speaking against homosexual lobbying groups. In one instance, a Protestant pastor in Alberta named Stephen Boissoin was told to pay a fine and write a renunciation of his views in a local paper. He was also ordered to never speak or write on the topic again. The ruling was overturned but only after more than seven years of legal harassment.[25] Whatever stand you take on the issue of homosexual rights, you have to admit that this is intolerance at its finest. (Ironically, the person in charge of the Human Rights Commission for this case also dismissed a complaint about a rock band with the lyrics "kill the Christian" in one of its songs.)[26]

8. Relativism destroys faith.

As we mentioned, it seems that most people today are under the false impression that if something is scientifically verifiable, it is objectively true, whereas everything else is only "subjectively true" (that is, sentiment or opinion). Such a belief reduces God from the status of actual living Being to personal sentiment that can legitimately vary from person to person.

Because of this demotion, relativists are able to say things like "Jesus is God *for you*, but Vishnu is God *for someone else*." By this, they mean not only that people see God differently but that God is, in fact, different for each person, as if each person is able to create his or her own deity based on his personal tastes, much in the same way that he would craft his own drink at Starbucks. There's a joke that the main difference between humans and God is that God never thinks he's us. By subjectifying God, relativism sets us up as creators of God rather than God as the Creator of us.

This idea is incompatible with the notion of God as an actual Being. If God is someone or something that each person creates—rather than someone we discover or someone who seeks us out—then he is no more *real* than a creation of a person's imagination. He is reduced to a mere projection from the mind of the believer or group of believers. However, if an intelligent and personal God really exists (as over 95 percent of the world's population would contend),[27] then he has attributes that our individual or collective opinions don't create or change, just as you have attributes that aren't changed by what people believe about you. Unlike make-believe characters, a *real* God would be a Being who exists independent of what we think of him and with attributes that our beliefs don't affect. This means that some people believe things about God that are wrong.

Coming to know, love, and follow the living God is the goal of faith. Such a relationship is impossible if God is not viewed as a Being who is independent of the believer's imagination. The believer may still go through the motions of religious practice for the sake of tradition or nostalgia, but he does so no longer in an attempt to understand and conform to a divine Being who exists beyond himself. For the relativist, the outer shell of faith may remain intact, but at its core, it has rotted away.

I just laid out for you why relativism is wrong and followed that up with a handful of ways that it's destructive to the world. But even if you *want* to agree with me, if you're convinced that relativism is the only way to achieve tolerance and that belief in objective truth is the root of all cruelty, I won't be able to change your mind.

You see, many are convinced that relativism is the glue that holds a pluralistic society together and that without it we'd dissolve into intolerant, warring clans. For this reason an argument for absolute truth is often perceived as an argument for Nazi-era intolerance. Naturally, such an argument is rejected even if it seems logical.

What is tolerance?

Tolerance is the one virtue a relativist society seems to value. Purity, piety, temperance, wisdom, and courage are all optional. But tolerance is taught from a young age and is expected of everyone. That would be a good thing if we all knew what tolerance was. Relativists seem to think that tolerance means not strongly disagreeing with anyone on moral or religious issues. In other words, what was previously called *disagreement* is now often labeled *intolerance*—or worse.

But the irony of calling someone intolerant for saying, "I'm right and you're wrong" is that such a statement is a prerequisite for tolerance. Tolerance is enduring ideas or actions that you don't agree with. So to be able to tolerate something, you first have to disagree with or dislike it! No one ever has to tolerate a beautiful sunny day. He has to tolerate the rain. Intolerance then, is a refusal to put up with something you disagree with.

Intolerance can be helpful at times, for instance, to preserve public safety (e.g., we don't tolerate murder), to preserve the integrity of a specific organization (e.g., you'll be fired from your post with the Democratic Party if you're an outspoken Republican), or to raise children with certain expectations (e.g., a good parent won't tolerate a child hitting his siblings).

Intolerance can be harmful if it's used to censor ideas, coerce people into agreeing with you, or if it takes the form of violence. When I talk about intolerance in this booklet, I'll be referring to its dark side.

Many seem to think that relativism is the only thing that can save the world from this type of intolerance. I'd argue that nothing could be further from the truth.

But hasn't relativism proven to help everyone get along in a pluralistic society?

Recent history has shown us that relativists can be more intolerant than those who believe in absolute truth. Take Adolf Hitler, for example, who said, "There is no such thing as truth, either in the moral or in the scientific sense."[28] Hitler's ally Benito Mussolini, the fascist dictator of Italy, is another clear-cut example of an intolerant relativist. Early in his political career, he wrote:

> Everything I have said and done in these last years is relativism, by intuition. From the fact that all ideologies are of equal value, that all ideologies are mere fictions, the modern relativist infers that everybody has the right to create for himself his own ideology, and to attempt to enforce it with all the energy of which he is capable. If relativism signifies contempt for fixed categories and men who claim to be the bearers of an objective immortal truth, then there is nothing more relativistic than fascism.[29]

Since Mussolini didn't recognize any higher reality—moral or religious—to which he should conform, he invented his own moral code and enforced it on everyone he could. After all, as long as he was in alignment with his own values, what objective standards did he have to restrain himself with?

To be fair, the average relativist wouldn't go as far as Hitler or Mussolini, but the modern world is increasingly full of examples of intolerance for those who believe in objective truth:

- Regular lawsuits backed by the ACLU to forcibly squash any mention of God out of the public square to cater to a few intolerant atheists[30]
- The college student in California who was threatened with expulsion after she said a prayer for a sick teacher on campus with his consent[31]
- A civil rights organization that protested a statue of Jesus found on the floor of the ocean[32]
- The Christian print-shop owner in Toronto who was fined for choosing not to print promotional materials for a gay and lesbian group[33]
- The attacks on conscientious objection rights that currently allow Catholic doctors and hospitals to refuse to participate in providing abortions[34]

Disagreeing and speaking out is not intolerant. Fining those you disagree with, threatening to force them to act against their conscience, and pushing all signs or expressions of their beliefs out of the public square is intolerant. The more that relativists gain political power, the less they tend to tolerate those with whom they disagree. It seems that a new *relativist* inquisition is underway. And, of course, it is being carried out in the name of tolerance!

But isn't religious absolutism the greatest cause of intolerance?

No. The vast majority of the 6 billion-plus people on the earth are members of a religion. Very few of them are suicide bombers. In the current cultural climate, it is also important to note that among the world's one billion-plus Muslims, a small minority are radical expansionists. In fact, average Muslims who are trying to live peaceful lives are the primary victims of such extremism.

People have committed extreme acts of violence in the name of God, but the source of their violence is not the fact that they are absolutists or realists (meaning that they claim to know *the* truth in faith and morals) but the radical things they believe or their skewed interpretation of otherwise peaceful doctrines. The majority of absolutists are not committing acts of savagery in the name of religion; to the contrary, even though faith may cause disagreements, it also often motivates charity and social order, which are necessary for the rights of individuals to be upheld.

Let's consider a "religious absolutist" whom most people remember: Mother Teresa. She believed in Jesus Christ with all the tenacity that any suicide bomber ascribes to his beliefs. She believed beyond the shadow of a doubt that she was right and other faiths were wrong when it came to the divinity of Jesus Christ. But could you imagine her walking into a crowd of Hindus and blowing herself up because of it or new videos being found and released on YouTube of her kneeing a poor Indian in the face because he didn't accept the message of Christianity? The idea is ridiculous. Her faith motivated her to a life of service to everyone regardless of creed or lifestyle—from feeding Hindus living in the slums of Calcutta to starting New York City's first AIDS hospice and much more.

Recent history has shown that a lack of faith has the potential to lead to just as much violence, if not more, than faith can. It may seem that if we could just "imagine there's no heaven . . . no hell below us . . . no religion too," we could "live life in peace," but the 20th century proved John Lennon's dream wrong time and again. People who imagined that there was no heaven, hell, or religion in the 20th century made many of the crimes committed in the name of faith look like child's play. Take communism, for instance, with its strong commitment to atheism. In one small communist country alone, Cambodia, 1.7 million persons died at the hands of the government from 1975 to 1979, with entire families, including infants, being put to death by the tens of thousands if they were a perceived threat to the Communist Party.

An honest look at history shows that religious absolutism doesn't necessarily make a person intolerant, nor does a lack thereof. It depends on *what* a person believes, not *if* he believes. In fact, faith has actually increased tolerance in the Western world.

How has Christianity contributed to a society of tolerance?

Jesus' death on the cross is the most radical revelation of human dignity that we find in any belief system. Christianity teaches that each person is of such great worth that God himself died for him. This revelation of the dignity of all people, great and small, has tremendous implications that we see play out in the history of Europe.

We could argue that the value we place on tolerance and the belief we have in the rights of the individual in Western culture can be traced back to its Judeo-Christian heritage more than to its pagan roots. The pagan world in which Christians first found themselves was extremely vicious. War, murder, gladiatorial contests, and public capital punishment were all a familiar part of life. A Roman father, whose rights were nearly absolute, could leave his child in the snow to die with no consequences. Simply put, if it weren't for Christianity, you'd be watching slaves from foreign lands in live glad-iator contests with your children on prime-time TV![35]

Despite attempts in most history text books to re-duce the historical contribution of Christianity to the Crusades and the inquisition, tolerance and human rights in general grew from within the Christian com-munity, even if this wasn't always perfectly lived out. The Catholic Church invented the hospital system and public universities, preserved the classics from bar-barian raiders, commissioned most of the art you can see in Europe, and is still the largest charitable and educational institution on earth today. Christian so-ciety, when true to its ideals, puts mankind first and ensures that technology, art, science, government, and education serve man, not the other way around. This recognition of the preeminence of man's place in the universe and of the dignity of each person is the basis of tolerance.

Whether you're Christian or not, you're still enjoy-ing the fruits of Judeo-Christian culture. To deny this is to have a biased view of history.

So then what do you make of all the examples throughout history of intolerant Christians?

We cannot deny instances of intolerance in Christian history. Pope John Paul II wrote of "painful chapter[s] of history to which the sons and daughters of the

Church must return with a spirit of repentance . . . [where] acquiescence [was] given, especially in certain centuries, to *intolerance and even the use of violence* in the service of truth."[36] We can highlight a few of the best-known examples. Take the inquisition (or more specifically, the infamous Spanish Inquisition, which was controlled by the Spanish monarchy). Or Europe's infamous witch hunts. Or the long period of wars known as the Crusades, for instance. Crusades were often justifiable and even successful in their intent to liberate Christian cities and churches that had been conquered, but sadly, it isn't hard to find records of Crusader brutality and intolerance in the name of Roman Catholicism, even toward Eastern Christians.

But a fair look at history shows that violence was not the overarching story of Christianity. The Catholic world was not won by the sword but by convincing preaching and charitable works. This is not the author's opinion. It is historical fact. Christianity spread most quickly when it was on the receiving end of the sword—which it has been countless times and still is today in many countries.

As the Catholic Church has grown, its teaching on tolerance has only become clearer. Past examples of intolerance have been officially and openly condemned.

We can only hope and pray that nations that still suppress religious freedom in the name of atheistic communism or Islam have a similar maturation and join the modern world in this regard. Going to some churches in China or North Korea can land you in jail. Converting to Christianity in Saudi Arabia, Afghanistan, and other countries is still a death sentence. Many are not aware of this widespread persecution. Sadly, there is little press or protest from the West when Christians are the brunt of intolerance.

Wouldn't Christians be intolerant today if they had enough power?

Many fear the dawn of a Christian theocracy in America. Rabbi James Rudin wrote in his book *The Baptizing of America: The Religious Right's Plans for the Rest of Us* that if Christians gained enough power,

> all manifestations of public homosexual or lesbian acts—including holding hands or kissing—would be subject to a fine and a jail sentence. . . . All government employees—federal, state, and local— would be required to participate in weekly bible [sic] classes in the workplace, as well as compulsory daily prayer sessions. . . . [Christians] seek to control what takes place in every room of the American mansion: the bedroom, the hospital and operating room, the news and press room, the library room, the courtroom, the schoolroom, the public room, and the workroom—the major facets of American society.[37]

But modern history shows that such fears are not grounded in reality. It could be argued that 60 years ago, Christians held a strong upper hand in American society. Prayer was commonplace in schools. Manger scenes were erected in public, and no one complained about being "disturbed" by baby Jesus. Sculptures of the Ten Commandments were displayed in public and no one was offended. Yet no one remembers the great American theocracy that was throwing people of other faiths or lifestyles in jail. It didn't exist.[38] To the contrary, Christians in recent history displayed, far better than many other cultures have, that it is very possible to disagree with others and remain tolerant, even if you are a majority.

How do you explain why religious people are always trying to legislate their morality? Isn't that intolerant?

Newsflash: Every law is the legislation of morality! And since no moral "rule" is respected by 100 percent of a population, every law is the imposition of a moral code that is recognized by a particular group within society (usually the majority) on everyone else.

If Christians were trying to legislate *religion*—for instance, making Sunday church attendance compulsory—that would be wrong. Forced faith, like forced love, isn't real, and it violates a person's freedom and dignity.[39] But if Christians try to legislate moral codes that are logical, are based on natural law (our innate sense of right and wrong), and uphold the common good, they shouldn't be silenced just because those laws also correspond to principles found in their faith. The attempt to do so is anti-religious bigotry.

Isn't it intolerant to exclude others, as many religious organizations do?

If by "intolerant" you mean "bigoted" or "cruel," no!

All groups, from the local yacht club to your local Catholic school, have guidelines. Without such guidelines, codes of conduct, or core beliefs, there is no definable group. At times, these principles demands exclusion. Excluding people from a group who don't share the beliefs or interests upon which the group is founded isn't necessarily intolerance. It's safe to say that the Gay, Lesbian, and Straight Education Network (GLSEN) would not accept my archbishop as a member unless he renounced the beliefs he's stated so publicly on same-sex marriage. But this type of exclusion is not intolerance in the negative sense of the word. It is simply a group being true to the principles that make it what it is.

So excluding people from a group for rejecting its core beliefs is not intolerant. But it is intolerant to force others to join a group or abide by its guidelines if they don't agree with them. Conversely, it is intolerant for non-members to force a group to abandon its core beliefs so that anyone can join it, attend its institutes of learning, or be married in its churches. GLSEN should be free to define itself, and so should the Catholic Church. There is room for peacefully, respectfully disagreeing organizations within the free world—even if those disagreements are strong.

Speaking of that, why is the Catholic Church so intolerant of homosexuals?

Like I said, disagreement is not the same thing as intolerance. The Church teaches very clearly that homosexual activity violates both natural and divine law. But the Church is also clear in its teaching about tolerance. According to the *Catechism of the Catholic Church*, people with same-sex attraction "must be accepted with respect, compassion, and sensitivity. Every sign of unjust discrimination in their regard should be avoided."[40]

But didn't Jesus accept everyone exactly as they were?

Jesus did accept people as they were, but he also challenged them to change their lives. These two aspects of his ministry stand in contradiction only if you fail to grasp what motivated his interactions with others: love.

Jesus Christ was so welcoming that it shocked the people of his day and would probably scandalize some of his followers today. He ate and drank with sinners. In other words, he was able to hang out with completely non-religious people without scaring them away.

On the other hand, Jesus was also extremely challenging to those he welcomed. Like any religious leader throughout history, Jesus invited people to live in a certain way. His demands actually exceeded those of the religious leaders of his time—not in exterior requirements but in an interior code with the highest demands. For instance, he likened anger to murder and lust to adultery with one's heart. He violently flipped over the money-changers' tables in the temple. He warned people about the fires of hell. He called the hypocrites of his day "whitewashed tombs," beautiful on the outside and full of death within. Yes, he saved the adulterous woman who was about to be killed for her crime with the famous words "Let he who is without sin throw the first stone at her." But he also told her, "Go and sin no more." (See John 8:1-11 for the full story.)

People tend to react harshly when the Catholic Church takes a firm stance on a moral issue, often asking, "What would Jesus do?"—as if sticking to a high ethical standard would be foreign to the mind of Christ. I'm guessing many of these people have never picked up a Bible.

Jesus Christ loved everyone enough to accept them as they were. Immoral behavior being as damaging as it is, he also loved them too much to let them stay that way.

Jesus taught his followers to do as he did: to welcome everyone but also to teach about sin, since love demands warning people about what can hurt them. Furthermore, the ideals set forth in Scripture challenge us to judge actions without judging people. Since we cannot see into a person's soul as God can, he alone reserves the role of judge for himself, giving us the mandate to love everyone without distinction or conditions. But this mandate to love is not at odds with the mandate to speak with clarity about moral issues or to challenge people to change the way they act when necessary.

Furthermore, the mandate to speak out about moral issues is not at odds with the command to never judge. In a relativistic society that confuses moral choices with personal expressions lacking any objectivity, many assume that judging a moral action is the same as judging a person. But saying that someone's action is wrong is not the same as saying that the person is bad.

Was Jesus tolerant?

If you believe he is who he claimed to be, then you'd agree that Jesus is the most tolerant man who ever lived. The all-powerful Son of God allowed himself to be tortured and prayed for forgiveness for his executioners. He instructed his followers to do what he did to the point of serving, forgiving, and even loving our enemies—a seemingly impossible command (although it might seem easy to you, until you have an enemy to love). There is simply no more radical form of tolerance or stricter command to love than this found in any other sacred text.

But isn't the belief that all non-Christians go to hell the ultimate and final intolerance?

Some Christian denominations believe this. Most do not. The Catholic Church, which comprises over one billion of the world's two billion Christians, does not teach that all people from other religions end up in hell.

The official teaching of the Church is that a person who doesn't know or hasn't been convinced about Jesus but has tried his best to follow God as he knows him—note: I didn't write, "tried his best to be nice": Hitler was nice to people he loved—can get into heaven through Jesus in a way that only God knows.[41] This teaching is based on our knowledge that God is fair and just, that he wants everyone in heaven, and that he is able to work outside of the ordinary parameters that he set up for us to be saved: belief in Jesus followed by baptism and a Christian life.

Even though not all Christians believe you have to be registered in a church to enter heaven, they still feel obliged to tell the world about Jesus.[42] Christians evangelize because they claim to know the ordinary and surest way that God has revealed for someone to arrive safely in heaven, because he commanded his followers to do so (evangelization is not an optional part of Christianity), and, most of all, because some news is just too good to keep to oneself. Non-Christians: If you truly believed that God loved us enough to become one of us and that his Resurrection is a proof for our pending eternal bliss, wouldn't you tell everyone you could? Seen in this light, the invitation of Christians should not be misconstrued as coercion. In the words of Pope John Paul II, "the Church proposes, she imposes nothing."[43]

It sure seems like an imposition sometimes.

Sometimes conscience might feel like it's imposing on us when we hear a moral or religious proposition. If you want to silence that voice, you're free to try, but please don't silence me! I'm just proposing.

Let's move on. What does motivate authentic tolerance?

The modern world thinks that relativism is the key

to tolerance—that is, if we abandon the thought that some ideas are right and others are wrong, *then* we can all get along. But I already showed how relativism can produce the polar opposite of tolerance because it removes objective reasons for people to practice self-restraint against those they disagree with.

In addition to this, relativism is not the "cure" for intolerance because it will simply never be accepted by absolutists who are intolerant. Try setting up an inclusivity workshop in the mountains of Afghanistan to convince members of the Taliban that there's really no difference among Christian, Jewish, or Islamic beliefs. You won't get very far—no matter how much multicolored yarn you bring with you to illustrate your point.

So what can cure intolerance? I argue that the most tolerant person is a realist (that is, someone who recognizes that there are objective religious and ethical facts) who recognizes that intolerance is wrong.

The Second Vatican Council taught very clearly about tolerance:

> We cannot truly call on God, the Father of all, if we refuse to treat in a brotherly way any man, created as he is in the image of God. Man's relation to God the Father and his relation to men his brothers are so linked together that Scripture says: "He who does not love does not know God" (1 Jn 4:8). . . . The Church reproves, as foreign to the mind of Christ, any discrimi-

nation against men or harassment of them because of their race, color, condition of life, or religion.[44]

Such a clear teaching that intolerance is a moral evil should come from religious leaders of every faith.

This message also needs to come from secular activists whose followers, when they gain enough power, tend to suppress those with whom they disagree. For instance, some of the more radical pro-gay marriage activists would like the government to *force* religious organizations to change their teaching and practice on sexual ethics to support gay marriage or adoption—or else risk lawsuits or the loss of their tax exempt status for "hate speech." This goes beyond activism to coercion and intolerance.

So we've pointed out how relativism leads to tenuous tolerance at best and how only belief in objective truth has the potential to guarantee real and lasting tolerance. Hopefully we've removed enough of your fears about realism to make you comfortable digging into our next discussion: how you *can* know the answers to the most important questions with certainty—questions about faith, morals, and the meaning of life.

Why do we need certainty about matters of faith and morals?

The more important something is, the more certainty we need to have about it. For example, if monosodium glutamate bothers your stomach, it would be a good idea to check with the waiter at a Chinese restaurant to see if there is any in what you are about to order. But let's raise the stakes—if you were allergic to MSG and it would send you into anaphylactic shock, you would probably want to see the ingredients yourself before eating. You'd want a high degree of surety if the meal could kill you.

The stakes are high when it comes to the meaning of life (faith) and how we should live it (morals). Such things cut to the very heart of the purpose of our existence and how we should live it out. Only a high degree of surety about these things can give us the confidence we need to face life with a firm sense of purpose and death with hope.

But with all the various views about God and how we should live, how can anyone claim to know the truth?

Many people stop at that question, as if the multitude of arguments and viewpoints excuses us from the responsibility of finding the correct answers. When it comes to the most profound, important questions about the meaning of life, you had better look into the evidence and find solid answers, or you might be missing the purpose of your existence.

Answers can be found to questions of faith and morals. And even though the answers can't be verified scientifically, they can be verified logically.

I'm a scientist. When I talk about truth, I'm talking about science. You're talking philosophy and religion. We're speaking on two totally different planes. We can't even debate!

Truth means the same thing no matter what we're talking about. As we stated above, truth is "being in accord with fact or reality."

Whether we're talking biology or philosophy, we find truth by observing data and making logical conclusions about it. If it's physical data, you call your observations and conclusions *physics*. If it has to do with numbers, you call it *math*. If you're observing moral experiences, you call it *ethics*. If it's information about God, you call it *theology*. But in each case, your brain is working through data to make conclusions and find truth.

Is there a difference between data you can put under a microscope and data of a more purely philosophical nature? Sure there is, but that doesn't make one science more reliable than the other. Concepts can be just as reliable as the stuff in your petri dish. For instance, you'll probably never be able to verify physically that 10 trillion plus 10 trillion equals 20 trillion. You'd need a *huge* counting board. But you know conceptually that the answer is true. Likewise, great minds throughout history from Aristotle (ancient Greek philosopher) to Fred Hoyle (20th-century astronomer and ex-atheist) to Thomas Aquinas (medieval theologian) have deduced from what we can observe physically and philosophically that there is an "unmoved mover,"[45] a "superintellect,"[46] or a "God"[47] that we cannot see.

When it comes to ethics, one way we can make strong arguments is by reasoning through the "data" of moral experiences.[48] We can know that some choices are noble and good because almost everyone perceives them that way. We can know that some things are wrong because people universally recoil at them. For instance, it's safe to say that murder is wrong because human beings almost universally know it is by intuition. Does it seem a little subjective to make moral judgments based on our collective human experience? Maybe. But it's no more subjective than saying that we know an apple is red because nearly everyone sees red when they look at it. Of course, someone who is colorblind will see green, but his perception is wrong. And someone who is brainwashed might think murder is acceptable, but he too is wrong.

So my question for the scientists who think that only material data can be seen as "evidence" is this: Why do you accept data and make conclusions about the physical world but not about more important things, like who God is or how you should live? Why limit your discoveries about the universe to the reality inside a petri dish? You study the matter of the universe, but you're missing the meaning.

I guess I'm just skeptical of things that can't be scientifically verified.

When someone thinks that we can never know anything of a spiritual nature with surety, we call that person a skeptic. Some are skeptics because they refuse to recognize anything immaterial as evidence for truth.

For many people, skepticism is far more than an intellectual stance. It's a rejection of a claim even if there's enough evidence to support it. Such skepticism is an unnatural posture to take toward people or concepts and is more a sign of a wounded spirit than of genius. After years in youth ministry, I've found that all of the logical answers in the world cannot help a person believe if he has a hard time trusting his own dad, for example. Sometimes confronting such foundational trust issues can help someone break out of skepticism.

It just seems so closed-minded to say you're right and everyone else is wrong.

"Closed-minded" is merely a negative way of saying *convinced*. In the words of G. K. Chesterton, "The object of opening the mind, as of opening the mouth, is to shut it again on something solid."[49] It's a good thing to close your mind once you find something worth closing it on.

So you Christians think that the rest of the world is flat-out wrong?

The claim to be 100 percent right about God is not the same as saying everyone else is 100 percent wrong. The Catholic Church claims to have the fullness of truth about God, but it does not claim that every other faith is entirely wrong.

Regarding the truth and nobility of other religions, the Church officially teaches the following:

> The Catholic Church rejects nothing that is true and holy in [other] religions. She regards with sincere reverence those ways of conduct and of life, those precepts and teachings which, though differing in many aspects from the ones she holds and sets forth, nonetheless often reflect a ray of that Truth which enlightens all men.[50]

And since there are truths to be found in other faiths, the Church recognizes that they can lead people to God and help them to encounter him in various ways.[51]

It is also common today to find religious leaders in dialogue and working together for the common good whenever possible. Pope Benedict XVI recently encouraged interreligious dialogue that would "enable different religions to come to know one another better and to respect one another, in order to work for the fulfillment of man's noblest aspirations, in search of God and in search of happiness."[52]

In some ways, all people of faith are on the same "team," running the same race toward the same God. Our posture as Christians should not be *over* them, because of our claim to know the truth, but rather walking toward God *with* them. This certainly seems to be Pope Benedict XVI's attitude.

But this respect for other faiths isn't the same as religious indifferentism. In the same speech, Pope Benedict XVI continued, "Indeed, [the Church] proclaims, and ever must proclaim Christ 'the way, the truth, and the life' (Jn 14:6), in whom men may find the fullness of religious life, in whom God has reconciled all things to himself."

The religions of the world are the story of our search for God, which arises from our nature as religious creatures, made by God and for God. Christians claim to know the story of God's search for man—to the point where he becomes one of us and tells us to our faces who he is, and in so doing, reveals who we are. So, while other faiths provide glimpses of God, Jesus reveals the whole picture.

So in short, the Christian's claim to be 100 percent right about God should not be equated with the claim that everyone else is 100 percent wrong. And it certainly shouldn't be confused with a disrespect for other people. Saying someone is wrong is not the same as saying he is unholy. Nor is theological correctness the same as holiness. The devil, for instance, is an expert in theology.

Doesn't it smack of pride to claim to know the truth?

Not as much as it smacks of pride to claim you can create your own truth—your own moral and spiritual universe. Not as much as it smacks of pride to assume that most of the human race throughout history has been wrong until the recent wave of "open-mindedness." And not as much as it smacks of pride to reduce revelations from God or from nature to the level of your individual opinion, as if human thought is that weighty. Those who believe in objective truth have the humility to seek the truth and attempt to conform to it when they find it. It's hard to conceive of a prouder approach to philosophy and theology than relativism.

Doesn't it seem to limit God in all his vastness to try to box him into one faith like Christians do?

Holding that we can't know God clearly enough to distinguish between true and false opinions about him seems to go from *vast* to *vague*. Strangely, in our relativist culture, if a spiritual concept is vague and hard to grasp, we conclude that it must be because it is profound. Contrarily, if a spiritual concept is black and white and crystal clear, we label it overly simplistic and narrow.

Christians believe that "God is love" (1 Jn 4:8). His becoming man and dying for us makes sense only in the logic of love. Far from this being a "limiting" definition, there is nothing more vast and profound than love. We can argue that no other faith makes a more sublime claim about who—or what—God is. And if God is love, then, despite all his vastness, wouldn't he reveal himself to us in ways that were clear and easy to grasp? That's what Jesus is: God with a face and a name speaking in human words. This self-revealing love of a transcendent God is far more profound and vast than the depiction of a vague, amorphous, impersonal, divine mass that has never cared enough for the people he made to reveal himself clearly to them.

But in the end, doesn't diversity strengthen us? And won't that be weakened if everyone thinks as you do about faith and morals?

In some ways, the co-existence of many cultures is a great strength of the modern world. It has given birth to nations that thrive in countless ways because of their creativity and openness to ideas. It inspires intelligent dialogue, challenges us to charity and understanding, and helps us to appreciate the common humanity that unites us all. But paradoxically, relativism destroys authentic diversity!

A world where people openly and honestly disagree is diverse. A world that mandates unity through *conformity* to relativism—and accuses people of bigotry for disagreeing with others—is far from diverse.

A relativist society sees all religious worldviews as equal and would suppress any person of faith who sees himself as more "right" than another. Such a society may have many churches, but in the end, each person is just a member of the "church of relativism"—holding the same central dogma that there is nothing of significant difference among faiths and that God is something each person makes up for himself instead of Someone each person discovers. There is nothing more monochromatic and boring than that. It's a cold December where both menorahs and Christmas trees are replaced with vague banners saying *hope* and *believe* but never saying why to hope or in what to believe.

True diversity is when we can strongly disagree with respect and charity.

My beloved brother-in-law is Jewish. I have no doubt that he thinks I'm dead wrong about Jesus. He isn't under the delusion that Jesus might be God for me, but someone entirely different for him. It's hard to be a relativist when it comes to a historical person. Jesus either is who he claimed to be or he's nuts. Of course, I'd claim that he absolutely is God and that my brother-in-law is dead wrong.

So we disagree about the person of Jesus. I'd assume that because of his affection for me, he'd be overjoyed if I came to share his Jewish faith. Likewise, I'd love if he became a Christian. That doesn't mean we hate each other or have a fist fight at every family gathering (not that the issue even comes up). To the contrary, we respect one another on our journey to God and can even pray together. That's a true example of unity in diversity. We don't need to be united in relativism to be united in brotherhood.

How can I know the truth about moral issues?

When considering whether an action is right or wrong, we should follow the law: natural law and divine law. Divine law, recognized by people of faith, is what God has revealed directly about how we should act. Natural law refers to the moral principles "written" in our very nature.

How can we know natural law? A better question would be "How can we not?" The Founding Fathers of the United States wrote that our basic human rights are "self-evident." It doesn't take intensive formation to grasp that people have the right to life, liberty, and the pursuit of happiness. Rather, it takes *de*-formation not to see it.

Thanks to natural law, most remote tribal cultures have "figured out" marriage and parental obligations and have frowned on behavior that undermines it. Familial obligations are written in the very nature of our procreating bodies.

Natural law is why murder has been the most highly punishable crime in almost all cultures throughout history. It violates the life we can simply "see" in a person. We instinctively recoil at it. We don't have to think about it.

Moral realism—a recognition that there are ethical principles that we all *should* live by—wasn't concocted by religious leaders. It's in our DNA. Children have an innate sense that there is a right and a wrong, a fair and an unfair etched into the foundations of the universe. After a child experiences the pain of playground injustice, it doesn't take him long to articulate that it is *bad* or *wrong* when someone steals his ball or slaps him in the face.

Relativism—a rejection of the notion that there are any *shoulds* or *should nots*—is an unnatural way of thinking. It has to be carefully taught to our children by the intellectual elite or forced on us by an oversized government that threatens citizens with penalties if they make an ethical claim that it has labeled as *bigotry*.

Because absolutism and natural law are such a part of the human experience, relativism has dominated only a small portion of human history, and it simply cannot dominate the world forever. If it succeeds at eventually tearing society apart (as it almost did in Mussolini's day), new realists will rise from the ashes.

It seems that people like you are trying to turn back the clock. Isn't relativism just about

us growing beyond antiquated moral views?

Relativism doesn't represent a growth from anti-quated views. It represents a total demolition of the human race's entire approach to ethics throughout history, replacing it with a flawed philosophy—the new "golden rule" that there are no rules.

As far as moral views becoming "antiquated": Words like *antiquated* should be used for things like toasters. Words like *right* and *wrong* should be used for ideas. If they're wrong, then they should be thrown out because they were always wrong. If they're right, then they should be even more trusted if they've stood the test of time. The passage of time doesn't make an ethical concept wrong or obsolete. You don't use ethics to tell time. Using a clock to judge moral issues is just as foolish.

Of course, in some areas the latest discoveries have replaced old ideas. You wouldn't use a textbook from 1850 in your college biology class any more than you would go shopping for an antique microwave. But the truths identified in philosophy (and theology) are timeless. They can be polished, but they don't rust.

How can I come to know the truth in matters of faith?

There is more to faith than compiling enough logical or personal reasons to make a rational conclusion.

Reason can lead us to the threshold of faith. Reason can also help us understand the content of our faith after we've crossed that threshold. But reason can't cross the actual threshold for us. It takes more than being a theological genius to be a person of deep faith. That is because the object of faith is not a thing or a topic but a person—God. Faith is not a science but a relationship. This is why faith is brought about by an act of the will, not only of the intellect. As an analogy, let's look at marriage.

Rational thought can lead a man to rule out all other options and narrow his selection down to the one person he wants to marry, but in the end, the "I do" is an act of will, a decision to surrender to a person. You can't scientifically verify everything you know about that person, nor can all of your knowledge explain away her mystery, yet after you acquire enough "evidence," her beauty and goodness leads you to make the decision to give her your life.

In some sense faith, like marriage, is a blind leap, but this is not because the Faith is irrational but rather, *supra-rational*—that is to say, beyond the limits of reason. (There are parts of our universe that are beyond the limits of our sight. That doesn't mean they aren't there.) As important as it is to use your reason, you cannot fully grasp the God you are embracing any more than you can fully grasp a marriage into which you are jumping, but once you have enough evidence, you jump anyway.

Still, consider the fact that atheism requires a leap of faith as well. No atheist can scientifically verify that there is zero possibility that God exists or why, if there is no God, there is anything in the universe as opposed to nothing. Yet after making a few "discoveries," the atheist makes that leap of faith and decides that there is no God. Thus, both faith and a lack thereof involve an act of the will.

What rational support is there for belief in God?

We're diverting a bit from relativism, but we can do that for one or two questions.

With all due respect to atheists, atheism is about as foolish as a flea refusing to believe in a dog. In the words of Edwin Conklin, biologist and associate of Albert Einstein at Princeton University, "The probability of life originating from an accident is comparable to the probability of the unabridged dictionary resulting from an explosion in a print shop."[53] A single strand of your DNA is more complex than a dictionary. There might have been a big bang followed by billions of years of evolution, but the notion that this could all happen without some intelligent "oversight" is as silly as seeing a book and assuming there is no author simply because you haven't seen him with your own eyes. It's as silly as assuming that conditions could have existed, by chance, for a book to evolve from nothing if given enough time.

We can't claim to know why there is a God and a universe as opposed to nothing at all, but we can know if we see a book that there is an author, if we see a painting there is a painter, if we see a string of things that began there is an ultimate "beginning," and if we see a universe there is a Creator.

This is why all the philosophers of antiquity (some of the greatest minds ever to live) believed in God, most relativists believe in God, and, I would argue, many self-proclaimed atheists believe in God—they're just angry at him for one reason or another.

What makes you so convinced about Christianity?

If someone rises from the dead by his own power, I'll believe anything he says. The founder of Christianity rose from the dead. In the 19th century, the highly respected Harvard law professor Simon Greenleaf recognized that Christianity hinged on the belief in Jesus' Resurrection. If Jesus Christ, in fact, rose from the dead, that substantiates everything he claimed. If he did not, he was either an opportunistic liar or a lunatic who thought he was God. Greenleaf sought to prove that the Resurrection would never stand in a court of law—but he ran into a problem with his theory: He knew that an eyewitness is a sure way to close a case. In the case of the Resurrection, he found not only many eyewitnesses but also that they all were willing to be put to death rather than retract their testimony. (It's important to note that these eyewitnesses weren't just willing to die for a belief or a philosophy but for testifying to a specific event that they had seen: the Resurrection.) Ten of the apostles suffered gruesome deaths and one was exiled. In the end, Greenleaf became a Christian.[54]

What do you do when the faith you are so sure of is tested by adversity? How do you stay sure?

Tragedy is an inevitable part of life. If you haven't experienced one yet, you eventually will, because pain is unavoidable, and everyone dies. What's worse is that you will probably experience the death of loved ones before your own. (Sorry for the downer.) At a time like that you might be tempted to cry out "My God, where are you?" (Check out Matthew 27:46. The God of love has cried out the same prayer so you wouldn't have to alone.) How can you keep faith at a time like that? You can continue to *choose* to believe.

As we said above, the object of faith is not a topic but a Person, and because of that, faith is not just in your head but involves an act of the will. Your brain is finite. It can recall only a limited scope of information at a time. In the midst of tragedy, you can't remember every reason you have for faith or everything that has reinforced that faith over the years in one instant—just as a man faced with temptation can't recall in one instant all the wonderful things he's experienced in marriage. But like that faithful spouse, you can continue to choose faith in a loving Author of life over hopelessness.

Often in the light of faith, the chaos of tragedy starts to make sense somehow, or at least it becomes bearable and doesn't drain the meaning out of life. In the words of St. Augustine, "Do not seek to understand so that you may believe, but believe so that you may understand."[55]

Seven Ways to Battle Relativism

Okay, I'm convinced that I can know the truth and that it doesn't make me intolerant to say so. So how should I combat relativism?

Following are a few tips to help you combat relativism. Each tip is harder than the last, and the last one is seemingly impossible—but by far the most necessary.

1. Get a copy of this booklet (or my CD on relativism at chris-stefanick.com) in the hands of everyone you know! Put it on car windows. Leave a stack out

at your parish. Share them with your anthropology professor who is venturing over his head into the realm of philosophy and attempting to indoctrinate all your friends with relativism.

2. Do you really want to become an anti-relativist warrior? Read more about this topic. Check out Pope John Paul II's encyclical *The Splendor of Truth*, Fr. Thomas Dubay's book *Faith and Certitude*, and Peter Kreeft's book *A Refutation of Moral Relativism*.

3. You have stopped thinking like a relativist; now stop talking like one. When you talk about matters of faith and morals, communicate with conviction. Follow the example of St. John when he wrote, "[We proclaim to you] what we have heard, what we have seen with our eyes, what we looked upon and touched with our hands" (1 Jn 1:1). No one had the impression that he was conveying mere opinion or vague theory. He was communicating fact.

Along those lines, unless it's to strengthen your argument, avoid prefacing your statements with "the Church teaches," as if that were a disclaimer. Just state what is as if it were fact (because it is nothing less).

In the words of Pope John Paul II, our teaching must "continually separate itself from the surrounding atmosphere of hesitation, uncertainty, and insipidity."[56] (I'm not sure what that last word means, but I'm sure it's bad!) If you constantly present the faith as "our opinion," then you are not spreading Christianity but relativism.

4. If you're married, be a loving and faithful spouse and parent. While there are many sociological reasons for the rise of relativism, the breakdown of the family is one of them. People raised in a family that was built on shifting sands rather than solid rock often find it hard to put their full trust in a heavenly Father.

5. Be joyful. A society living under the dictatorship of relativism is unable to grasp the inherent meaning of life. Consequently, it may have many "fun" distractions, but it is noticeably lacking in real joy. Your joy will communicate clearly that you have found that life makes sense and that it is worth living. Seeing this, the world will hunger for what you have. So as bad as the world gets, don't become a whiner that no one wants to be around. Never forget to revel in what you have found. Remember, you are the only church some people may ever visit!

6. Speak the truth with love. I have no doubt that part of the reason the world has fallen into relativism is in response to people presenting the truth without love and mercy, which is a unique form of cruelty.

While your mind should close on truth when you find it, your heart should never close toward people. Never be short-tempered with people who don't see what you see. Never show contempt for them because of their beliefs or where they are in their life's journey. If you do, your sharing of the faith will strike people like a "noisy gong or clanging cymbal" (1 Cor 13:1). In other words, it will push them away. To share the truth about Christ effectively, you have to truly love people—not just loving them so that they might convert but wanting their conversion because you love them—to the point that you will continue loving them even if they persist in their sin, relativist views, disbelief, or whatever the case may be.

In the words of Pope John Paul II at the canonization of St. Edith Stein—a Catholic Carmelite nun who died in Auschwitz because of her Catholic faith and her Jewish descent—"Do not accept anything as the truth if it lacks love. And do not accept anything as love which lacks truth! One without the other becomes a destructive lie."[57] People today need the same type of response that Jesus gave to a broken world in A.D. 33 when perfect Truth hung on the cross in perfect Love. He never failed to stick to his principles and teachings—to the point that it got him crucified. Yet he never stopped loving, even those who killed him.

7. Those tips are minute in importance in comparison with my last "tip": Become Saint (your name here).[58] A world that is dominated by relativism has a hard time grasping logical presentations about relativism—or about anything at all, for that matter. Personal holiness is the ultimate argument that a spiritual reality exists that is as solid as the ground

under our feet and that, because of it, life is worth living even when it is difficult.[59]

It is holiness that enabled a woman who lived in poverty, chastity, and obedience while serving the poor in Calcutta, India, to become a household name in a world consumed with wealth, sex, and power. Holiness enabled an 82-year-old man with Parkinson's in a Roman outfit to draw larger crowds of teens than the hottest secular band ever could. Even those who love to hate the Catholic Church couldn't help but be moved by Mother Teresa and Pope John Paul II. The communist dictator Fidel Castro couldn't resist inviting John Paul II to Cuba—even though the pope was integral in helping topple communism in Poland!

Holiness is an irresistible force today, just as it was for Herod, who, despite the power and the carnal pleasures with which he surrounded himself, couldn't resist his attraction to a man clothed with camel's hair who lived on a steady diet of locusts. St. John the Baptist's words seared through Herod's life of luxury and left an indelible mark on his soul.

The "solution" to the problem of every age is ultimately the same. The same thing will win back the world today that won it over in the first place 2,000 years ago when a ragtag group of fishermen without any worldly power or means decided to leave everything to follow Jesus. Holiness. That is the silver bullet. Period. So when people who are choking on the fumes of relativism come near you, they should get a whiff of the rarified air of heaven and a glimpse into a world that makes sense. You are needed to become a spiritual furnace in an increasingly cold, dark world.

When Pontius Pilate asked Jesus, "What is truth?" he was looking into the face of the One who said, "I am the way, the truth, and the life." He didn't say, "I am a way, an opinion, and a lifestyle." Don't just talk about him: *Show* his face to the world today. I wish I could offer an easier solution, as this one requires your whole life, but there is none.

ENDNOTES

1   Zenit.org, "Cardinal Ratzinger Calls Relativism 'Greatest Problem of Our Time,'" September 26, 2003, accessed March 30, 2011, http://www.zenit.org/article-8266?l=english.

2   When we talk about relativism in this booklet, we're specifically talking about moral and religious relativism.

3   Joseph Ratzinger, homily, *Pro Eligendo Romano Pontifice*, April 18, 2005, accessed March 30, 2011, http://www.vatican.va/gpII/documents/homily-pro-eligendo-pontifice_20050418_en.html.

4   A more academic relativist might try to avoid this self-contradicting proposition by defining relativism as the philosophy that there is no absolute truth but only relative truth. While this statement avoids overtly contradicting itself, it is still flawed because the person making the statement is implying that what he's saying is absolutely, universally true. He's being inconsistent with himself.

5   Rudolph Giuliani, "Text: Giuliani at the United Nations" (speech, United Nations, New York, October 1, 2001), accessed March 30, 2011, http://www.washingtonpost.com/wp-srv/nation/specials/attacked/transcripts/giulianitext_100101.html.

6   Pope Benedict XVI, homily on the occasion of the Twenty-Third World Youth Day, July 20, 2008, accessed March 30, 2011, http://www.vatican.va/holy_father/benedict_xvi/homilies/2008/documents/hf_ben-xvi_hom_20080720_xxiii-wyd_en.html.

7   Etan Horowitz, "OMG! Clermont Girl Texts 35,000 Messages in 1 Month," *Orlando Sentinel*, January 14, 2009, accessed February 26, 2011, http://www.orlandosentinel.com/news/local/lake/orl-text1409jan14,0,5867250.story.

8   Pope John Paul II, address to the young people in Rizal Park, January 14, 1995, accessed March 30, 2011, http://www.vatican.va/holy_father/john_paul_ii/speeches/1995/january/documents/hf_jp-ii_spe_19950114_vigilia-manila-gmg_en.html.

9   Centers for Disease Control and Prevention, "Suicide: Facts at a Glance," Summer 2009, accessed March 30, 2011, http://www.cdc.

gov/violenceprevention/pdf/Suicide-DataSheet-a.pdf.

10 Pope Benedict XVI, address to the participants in the Ecclesial
    Diocesan Convention of Rome, June 6, 2005, accessed March
    30, 2011, http://www.vatican.va/holy_father/benedict_xvi/
    speeches/2005/june/documents/hf_ben-xvi_spe_20050606_
    convegno-famiglia_en.html.

11 Barack Obama, interview by Cathleen Falsani, CathleenFalsani.
    com, March 27, 2004, accessed March 30, 2011, http://
    cathleenfalsani.com/obama-on-faith-the-exclusive-interview/.

12 This is also the first commandment of the official Church of Satan
    founded by Anton LaVey: "Do what thou wilt shall be the whole
    of the law."

13 Robyn Lydick, "Becoming Jamie," *Highlands Ranch Herald*
    (Highlands Ranch, Colo.), February 29, 2008, accessed March
    30, 2011, http://www.coloradocommunitynewspapers.com/
    articles/2008/02/29/front%20page/19346255.txt.

14 Pope Benedict XVI, encyclical letter, *Caritas in Veritate*, 3.

15 Pope Benedict XVI, address to the participants in the Ecclesial
    Diocesan Convention of Rome.

16 Illustration from a Toastmasters speech by James Stefanick,
    spring 1996. *E pluribus unum* is the Latin phrase on the Great
    Seal of the United States.

17 Archbishop Charles J. Chaput, "The Captivity of 'Catholic'
    Witness," *First Things*, March 19, 2010, accessed March 30, 2011,
    http://www.firstthings.com/blogs/firstthoughts/2010/03/19/on-
    the-square-today-14/.

18 Pope John Paul II, encyclical letter, *Evangelium Vitae*, 20.

19 The Web site of NARAL Pro-Choice America (formerly the
    National Abortion and Reproductive Rights Action League) is
    simply www.prochoiceamerica.org, highlighting the centrality of
    "choice" to their cause. A bill recently pushed in the U.S. to end
    every state restriction on abortion is simply called the "Freedom
    of Choice Act," or "FOCA."

20 Pope John Paul II, encyclical letter, *Veritatis Splendor*, 84.

21 Lydia Saad, "More Americans 'Pro-Life' Than 'Pro-Choice' for
    First Time," Gallup, May 15 2009, accessed March 31, 2011, http://

www.gallup.com/poll/118399/more-americans-pro-life-than-pro-choice-first-time.aspx. The Gallup poll conducted May 7–10, 2009 found that 51 percent of Americans call themselves "pro-life" and 42 percent call themselves "pro-choice."

22 Steve Connor, "Britain's 'Father of IVF' Wins the Nobel Prize," *The Independent*, October 5, 2010, accessed March 31, 2011, at http://www.independent.co.uk/news/science/britains-father-of-ivf-wins-the-nobel-prize-2097650.html.

23 Pope John Paul II, speech upon his arrival at Denver's Stapleton International Airport for World Youth Day, August 12, 1993, accessed March 31, 2011, http://www.ewtn.com/library/YOUTH/JP2DEN1.TXT.

24 Canadian Human Rights Act, Section 13.1.

25 Thaddeus M. Baklinski, "Pastor Boissoin Exonerated: Judge Rules Letter on Homosexuality Not 'Hate' Speech," LifeSiteNews.com, December 4, 2009, accessed March 31, 2011, http://www.lifesitenews.com/news/archive/ldn/2009/dec/09120407.

26 Hilary White, "Human Rights Commission: 'Kill the Christian' Lyrics OK, but Criticize Homosexuality? No Way," LifeSiteNews.com, November 3, 2008, accessed March 31, 2011, http://www.lifesitenews.com/news/archive/ldn/2008/nov/08110303.

27 Only 2.32 percent of the World's population is atheist, according to a 2007 estimate cited by the CIA. Taken from *The World Factbook* on January 19, 2011.

28 William Donohue, *Secular Sabotage* (New York, N.Y.: FaithWords, 2009), 12. See also Carl Sagan, *The Demon-Haunted World* (New York, N.Y.: Random House, 1996), 261.

29 From *"Diuturna,"* 374–77, quoted in Peter Kreeft, *A Refutation of Moral Relativism* (San Francisco: Ignatius Press, 1999), 18.

30 Press release, "Indiana High School Student Fighting Graduation Prayer Tradition," ACLU, April 13, 2010, accessed March 31, 2011, http://www.aclu.org/religion-belief/indiana-high-school-student-fighting-graduation-prayer-tradition-0; press release, "ACLU Urges Supreme Court to Uphold Ruling Removing the Phrase 'under God' from Pledge of Allegiance Recited in Public Schools," ACLU, March 24, 2004, accessed March 31, 2011, http://

www.aclu.org/content/aclu-urges-supreme-court-uphold-ruling-removing-phrase-under-god-pledge-allegiance-recited-p. These are two of seemingly countless examples of the ACLU's efforts to scrub faith from the public square.

31 Dennis Evanosky, "CoA Prayer Lawsuit Can Move Forward," *Alameda Sun* (Alameda, Calif.), April 16, 2009, accessed March 31, 2011, http://www.alamedasun.com/index.php?option=com_content&task=view&id=5029&Itemid=10.

32 "This Week," *National Review*, June 11, 1990, 12.

33 LifeSiteNews.com, "Scott Brockie Loses Decision at Court of Appeals, on the Hook for $40,000," April 16, 2004, accessed March 31, 2011, http://www.lifesitenews.com/news/archive/ldn/2004/apr/04041604. Brockie served gay customers but was opposed to printing promotional materials for a gay activist group because of his religious beliefs. He was fined $5,000 and ended up paying $40,000 in legal costs.

34 Steven Ertelt, "Council of Europe Defeats Attack on Abortion Conscience Rights for Medical Staff," LifeNews.com, October 10, 2010, accessed March 31, 2011, http://www.lifenews.com/2010/10/10/int-1663/. See also Eamonn Mattheson, "Proposed Abortion Laws Threaten Doctors' Rights," ABC News (Australia), October 2, 2008, accessed March 31, 2011, http://www.abc.net.au/news/stories/2008/10/02/2379845.htm.

35 St. Telemachus's martyrdom led to the banning of gladiatorial contests by Emperor Honorius in A.D. 404.

36 Pope John Paul II, apostolic letter, *Tertio Millennio Adveniente*, 35.

37 Rabbi James Rudin, *The Baptizing of America: The Religious Right's Plans for the Rest of Us* (New York: Thunder's Mouth Press, 2006), 15, 18, 72–73, quoted in Donohue, *Secular Sabotage*, 33.

38 Donohue, *Secular Sabotage*, 33.

39 Second Vatican Council, *Dignitatis Humanae*, 2.

40 *Catechism of the Catholic Church*, 2358.

41 Ibid., 887; Second Vatican Council, *Lumen Gentium*, 16.

42 CCC 847.

43 Pope John Paul II, *Redemptoris Missio*, 39.

44 Second Vatican Council, *Nostra Aetate*, 5.

45 In book 8 of the *Physics*, Aristotle argues for the necessity of an "unmoved mover."

46 Fred Hoyle, "The Universe: Past and Present Reflections." *Engineering and Science* (November 1981), 8–12.

47 St. Thomas Aquinas, *Summa Theologiae* I:2–3. Here, St. Thomas lays out logical proofs for God's existence.

48 Kreeft, 54.

49 G. K. Chesterton, *Autobiography*. Collected Works Vol. 16, p. 212.

50 Vatican II, *Nostra Aetate*, 2.

51 Vatican II, *Lumen Gentium*, 16.

52 Pope Benedict XVI, meeting with the diplomatic corps to the Republic of Turkey, November 28, 2006, accessed April 3, 2011, http://www.vatican.va/holy_father/benedict_xvi/speeches/2006/november/documents/hf_ben-xvi_spe_20061128_diplomatic-corps_en.html.

53 *Reader's Digest*, January 1963, 92.

54 His work, *The Testimony of the Evangelists*, was published in 1846. I also use this argument in *Do I Have to Go: 101 Questions about the Mass, the Eucharist, and Your Spiritual Life*, though with somewhat different wording.

55 St. Augustine of Hippo, *Tractate* 29 on John 7:14–18, NewAdvent.org, accessed April 3, 2011, http://www.newadvent.org/fathers/1701029.htm.

56 Pope John Paul II, *Catechesi Tradendae*, 56.

57 Pope John Paul II, "Canonization of Edith Stein and Homily," *L'Osservatore Romano*, weekly edition in English, October, 14, 1998, 1, accessed April 3, 2011, http://www.ewtn.com/library/papaldoc/jp2stein.htm.

58 Kreeft, 174. This is also Kreeft's final piece of advice for battling relativism.

59 "Art and the saints are the greatest apologetic for our faith." Pope Benedict XVI, meeting with the clergy of the Diocese of Bolzano-Bressanone, August 6, 2008, accessed April 3, 2011, http://www.vatican.va/holy_father/benedict_xvi/speeches/2008/august/documents/hf_ben-xvi_spe_20080806_clero-bressanone_en.html.